· THE ·
LITTLE KITCHEN
COLLECTION

THE

CHOCOLATE

C O O K B O O K

Patricia Lousada

ILLUSTRATED BY AISLINN ADAMS

HarperCollins*Publishers*

First published in 1992 by The Appletree Press Ltd,
19-21 Alfred Street, Belfast BT2 8DL
Tel: +44 232 243074
Fax: +44 232 246756

THE CHOCOLATE COOKBOOK

For information address HarperCollins Publishers,
Inc., 10 East 53rd Street, New York, NY 10022.

HarperCollins books may be purchased for
educational, business or sales promotional use. For
information please write: Special Markets
Department, HarperCollins Publishers Inc., 10 East
53rd Street, New York, NY 10022.

First Edition

LIBRARY OF CONGRESS CATALOG CARD NUMBER:
92-52581

ISBN: 0-06-016903-6

92 93 94 95 96 10 9 8 7 6 5 4 3 2 1

Introduction

Chocolate came to Europe in the sixteenth century, brought to Spain by the explorer Cortez, who first drank it at the court of Montezuma. Thousands of years before this, Mayans and Incas were brewing it as a drink and using the beans as a currency between individuals and states. In the hands of the Spanish the drink was transformed by the addition of sugar and vanilla and soon became popular all over Europe. By the middle of the seventeenth century, chocolate houses were popular meeting places and Samuel Pepys in his Diary writes of enjoying *jocalatte*. Eating chocolate was first made by the Dutch in the early nineteenth century and shortly after that in Great Britain. Later in the century the formulas were refined by the Swiss who changed the then grainy texture into the smooth one so popular today.

Despite Madame de Sevigné's prediction in 1671 that chocolate would fall from fashion, it has continued to gain in popularity. When we want to provide a treat we think of chocolate. This little book is full of just such treats for many different occasions. Cakes for tea or birthdays and sumptuous terrines for elegant entertaining. The botanical name for the chocolate plant, *Theobrama cacao,* means "food of the Gods," but ordinary mortals seem to have been addicted to chocolate forever and it is likely that they will continue to be.

A word on ingredients. It is crucial to use the very best chocolate available. Use good semi-sweet or unsweetened chocolate with a minimum of 50% cocoa solids. Vanilla sugar is made by storing a few vanilla beans in a jar containing superfine sugar.

White Chocolate Terrine

Serve this terrine in slices surrounded by a bitter-sweet rich dark chocolate sauce. Even sceptics of white chocolate will find it delicious.

7 tbsp water
1 tsp of powdered gelatine
1¹/₂ cups heavy cream
2 tbsp glucose powder
10oz white chocolate, finely chopped
3 egg yolks
a thin genoise sponge cake, to cover top
pinch of salt
Chocolate sauce:
¹/₂ cup plus 2 tbsp water
¹/₂ cup superfine sugar
¹/₂ cup cocoa powder
Serves 10

Soak the gelatine in 3 tablespoons of cold water. Whip the cream to the soft peak stage and leave in a cool place. Bring the glucose and 4 tablespoons of water to a simmer, remove from the heat and stir in the gelatine and chocolate. Stir until the mixture is smooth. When the mixture is blood temperature, add the egg yolks and fold in the cream. Place the mixture in a 1 lb loaf pan (no need to grease it) and cover with the sponge, cut to fit. Place in the refrigerator and leave for 24 hours.

To unmold: Place the mold in very hot water for a few seconds and then turn out. Slice with a thin sharp knife heated in hot water and dried. Place a slice on individual serving plates and surround with some chocolate sauce. To make the sauce, simply dissolve the sugar in the water, bring to the boil and whisk in the cocoa.

Black and White Chocolate Terrine

A delicious double-chocolate terrine sandwiched with a thin layer of hazelnut meringue. It can be served in thin slices, either on its own or with a raspberry sauce.

Meringue:	5oz *white chocolate,*
³/₄ cup hazelnuts	*chopped*
1 tbsp flour	*1 egg yolk*
¹/₃ cup superfine sugar	6oz *semi-sweet*
oil for greasing	*chocolate, chopped*
2 egg whites	*6 tbsp unsalted butter,*
a pinch of salt	*cut into small pieces*
Chocolate creams:	*2 tbsp strong coffee*
1¹/₂ tsp gelatine	*1¹/₄ cups heavy cream*
6 tbsp water	*a pinch of salt*

Serves 12

For the meringue: Preheat the oven to 350°F. Lightly toast the nuts on a baking tray for 10 minutes. Rub the nuts in a towel to remove most of the skins. Grind the nuts with the flour and half of the sugar. Line a 7 x 10 inch shallow pan with oiled baking parchment. Whisk the egg whites with a pinch of salt until firm then whisk in the remaining sugar until stiff peaks form. Fold in the nut mixture and spread over the prepared pan. Bake for 20 minutes. Cool for a few minutes, then slip a knife around the edge, invert on to a wire rack and remove the pan. Peel off the paper when cool.

For the chocolate creams: Place the gelatine with 4 tablespoons of cold water in a cup and leave for 5 minutes. Place the cup in hot water and leave until the gelatine is dissolved. Melt the white chocolate in the top of a double saucepan then remove from the heat. Stir in the egg yolk, salt, half the dissolved gelatine, and 2 tablespoons of water. Place the mixture in the refrigerator to cool. Meanwhile melt the semi-sweet chocolate in the same way. Remove from the heat and stir in the butter, the remaining gelatine and coffee. Refrigerate while you whip the cream. Fold half the cream into the white chocolate mixture and half into the dark chocolate mixture. Line a hinged 3 x 10 inch loaf pan with plastic wrap. Cut the meringue into two lengths to fit the pan and place one layer in the tin. Spread the dark chocolate cream over the meringue. Set the other meringue over this and cover it with the white chocolate. Cover the pan with plastic wrap and refrigerate overnight. Remove the terrine from the pan and slice it with a thin sharp knife dipped into boiling water and then dried. Center the slices on individual plates and leave them in a cool place until ready to serve.

Quick Treat

This makes an excellent and very attractive dessert for a dinner party and the big plus is that you can whip it up in a matter of minutes.

1 lb unsweetened chocolate	3oz glacé cherries,
12 tbsp unsalted	chopped
butter, softened	2 tbsp cognac
pinch of salt	¾ cup heavy cream
12 petit buerre cookies	grated chocolate for
	decorating

Serves 12

Melt the chocolate in the top of a double boiler. Meanwhile cut the cookies into ½ in pieces. When the chocolate has melted, remove from the heat and beat in the butter, cognac, and salt. Stir in the cookies and cherries and turn into a 7 inch diameter shallow cake pan lined with baking parchment. Press the mixture into a smooth layer and refrigerate (or freeze if you are short of time) for at least 30 minutes. Slip a knife around the edge of the pan and turn out on to a serving plate. Cover the top with a layer of whipped cream dusted with grated chocolate. Delicious served with coffee.

Chocolate Rum Fondue

A must for chocolate lovers and a great conversation piece. Your guests create their own dessert by dipping fruit and cake into this warm rich fondue.

1 cup sugar
½ cup water
3oz semi-sweet chocolate, chopped
3½oz unsweetened chocolate, chopped
4 tbsp unsalted butter
2 tbsp whipping cream
3 tbsp of rum or fruit eau-de-vie
fresh strawberries, slices of fresh pear and cubes of cake
Serves 4

Place the sugar and water together in a small, heavy-bottomed saucepan. Bring gently to the boil, simmer for 3 minutes, then set aside. Melt both chocolates with the butter and cream in the top of a double saucepan filled with barely simmering water. Stir in the sugar syrup. Before serving, reheat in the top of a double saucepan and stir in the rum or *eau-de-vie*. Serve in a chafing or fondue dish with a plate of fruit and cake pierced with thin wooden skewers for dipping.

Chocolate Marquise

This certainly must qualify as one of the very best and most elegant of chocolate desserts. It has a melt-in-the-mouth consistency and a superb chocolate flavor. It is well worth making your own sponge fingers to enhance such a confection.

6oz semi-sweet chocolate
10 tbsp unsalted butter,
cut into small pieces
½ cup cocoa powder
2 eggs
⅓ cup superfine sugar

1–2 tbsp white rum
1½ cups heavy cream,
whipped
small cup of strong black
coffee, unsweetened
lady fingers

Serves 10

Line a 6½ inch diameter charlotte mold with plastic wrap, leaving an overlap around the edge to ease turning out. Melt the chocolate in the top of a double saucepan over hot but not boiling water. Whisk in the butter and then the cocoa and remove from the heat. Whisk the eggs and sugar over a bowl of hot water until the mixture is very thick and leaves a ribbon trail when the whisk is lifted. Using a metal spoon, fold the chocolate mixture into the eggs, then fold in the rum and whipped cream. Brush the lady fingers with the cold coffee and line the bottom and sides of the mold, cutting them to shape where necessary. Spoon in the chocolate mixture, cover with plastic wrap and refrigerate for several hours or overnight. Turn out and leave at room temperature for an hour before serving. Slice with a thin sharp knife dipped in hot water and then dried. The marquise will keep for 3–4 days if refrigerated.

Chocolate Roulade

6oz semi-sweet chocolate
3 tbsp water
2 tbsp cognac
5 eggs
³/₄ cup superfine sugar
confectioners' sugar
1¹/₂ cups whipping cream
Serves 8–10

Line a 13¹/₂ x 9¹/₂ inch shallow pan with non-stick baking paper.
Preheat the oven to 350°F. Melt the chocolate, water and liqueur
together in the top of a double saucepan over hot but not boiling
water. Separate the eggs, cracking the yolks into a large bowl and
the whites into another bowl. Add the sugar to the yolks and whisk
until pale in color. Stir in the melted chocolate. Whisk the egg
whites until stiff, then fold gently into the chocolate mixture, using
a metal spoon. Pour into the prepared tin spreading evenly with
a palette knife. Bake for 15 minutes. Remove from the heat, cover
with a sheet of wax paper and a damp cloth and leave overnight
or for several hours.

Turn the roulade out on to a sheet of wax paper that has been
well-dusted with confectioners' sugar. Peel away the baking
paper. Whip the cream and spread over the surface of the roulade.
Roll up using the sugared paper to help. Before serving dust with
confectioner's sugar and cut into slices with a hot sharp knife.

Chocolate Sin

A very special flour-less cake, light and moist and with the unique advantage of having one mixture serve as both cake and frosting.

10oz semi-sweet or
unsweetened chocolate
8 tbsp unsalted butter
5oz vanilla superfine
sugar (p. 3)
7 egg yolks
6 egg whites

1 tbsp crème de cacao,
or dark rum
pinch of salt
cocoa for dusting
1 cup
whipped cream to serve

Serves 10–12

Butter and flour an 8 inch cake pan and line the bottom with baking parchment. Preheat the oven to 325°F. Melt the chocolate and butter together in the top of a double saucepan set over a pan of hot but not boiling water. Meanwhile whisk the egg yolks and $2/3$ of the sugar until it is thick and light in color. Fold the chocolate mixture into the egg yolks and add the alcohol and a pinch of salt. Whisk the egg whites with another small pinch of salt until the soft peak stage is reached. Add the remaining sugar and continue to whisk until stiff peaks have formed. First fold a few large tablespoons of the whites into the chocolate mixture to lighten it before folding in the rest. Spoon about $3/4$ of the batter (refrigerate the rest) into the cake pan and smooth the top level with a spatula. Bake for 45 minutes. Leave in the pan for 10 minutes before running a knife around the edge and carefully turning out on to a wire rack. When the cake is cool, reverse it on to a serving dish. The top may be slightly cracked but this is normal. Cover the cake with the remaining chocolate mixture. Sift a fine layer of cocoa over the top before serving.

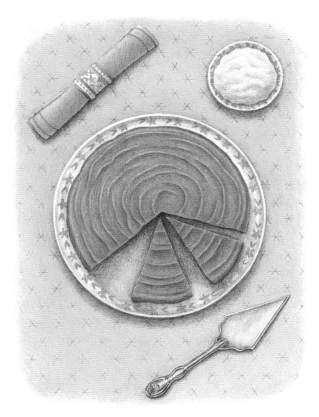

Chocolate Chestnut Mousse Cake

The flavors of chestnuts and chocolate go well together and in this recipe they combine to make an elegant and delicious dinner party dessert.

4oz semi-sweet chocolate
4 eggs separated
1 cup sugar
1 cup canned unsweetened chestnut purée
pinch of salt
1 tsp vanilla extract
½ cup plus 2 tbsp whipping cream
4 marrons glacé, finely chopped (optional)
cocoa powder
Serves 10

Line a 12½ x 9½ inch jelly-roll pan with wax paper. Preheat the oven to 350°F. Melt the chocolate in the top of a double boiler over hot, but not boiling water. Beat the egg yolks with ¾ of the sugar, then beat in the chestnut purée, vanilla, and melted chocolate. Sift the mixture into a clean bowl. Whip the egg whites and salt until stiff, add the remaining sugar and whisk until glossy. Using a metal spoon, fold a quarter of the egg whites into the chestnut mixture. Carefully fold in the rest of the whites and then spread over the prepared pan. Bake for 15–20 minutes. Leave in the pan to cool. The cake can be prepared to this stage 24 hours ahead of time. An hour or two before serving, whip the cream and fold in the marrons glacé. Cut the cake into 3 equal strips and sandwich with the cream. Sift a layer of cocoa over the top and serve in thin slices.

Scrumptious Chocolate Layer Cake

A delicious layer cake with lots of frosting and three thick layers of chocolate cake.

Cake:	Frosting:
8 tbsp unsalted butter, plus extra for greasing	8oz semi-sweet chocolate chopped
1 cup unsifted all-purpose flour	6 tbsp softened unsalted butter, diced
½ cup cocoa powder	3 eggs, separated
a good pinch of salt	1 cup whipping cream
6 eggs	3 tbsp superfine sugar
1 cup vanilla superfine sugar (p. 3)	

Serves 12

Preheat the oven to 350°F. Line 3 buttered and floured round 8 inch cake pans with baking parchment. Melt the butter over a very low heat, skim off some of the surface froth, discard it and set the butter aside. Sift the flour, cocoa, baking powder and salt together three times and set aside. Break the eggs into a large bowl, preferably a copper one and set over a pan of hot but not boiling water. Using an electric hand-held beater, whisk the eggs and vanilla superfine sugar for about 7 minutes or until the mixture has doubled in volume and is thick enough to leave a ribbon trail when the whisk is lifted. Sift the dry ingredients over the mixture by thirds, folding in each batch carefully with a large metal spoon, then fold in the melted butter. Divide the mixture between the prepared pans, smooth the surfaces with a spatula and bake for 25 minutes, or until the cakes shrink from the sides of the pan. Leave for 5 minutes and then turn out on to a rack to cool.

For the frosting: Melt the chocolate in the top of a double saucepan set over hot water. Whisk in the butter and egg yolks. Remove the pan from the water and leave to cool. Whip the cream and fold into the chocolate mixture. Whisk the egg whites until

they are stiff and then whisk in the sugar until the whites become glossy. Carefully fold this into the chocolate. Chill for about 15 minutes to thicken before spreading it between the layers and over the top and sides of the cake.

Brownie Layered Cream Cake

This cake came about by a happy accident. One day I made brownies in a hurry and added too much flour and cooked the mixture too long. The result was a cake that I rescued by slicing into layers and sandwiching with whipped cream. It became my children's favorite cake.

8 tbsp butter
1/2 cup cocoa powder, sifted
2 eggs
1 cup superfine sugar
1 tsp vanilla extract
scant 1/2 cup self-rising flour

scant 1/2 cup
 all-purpose flour
scant 2 cups heavy cream
Chocolate curls:
8oz semi-sweet chocolate
1 tbsp sunflower or
 groundnut oil

Serves 8–10

Grease an 8 inch round cake pan and line the bottom with buttered wax paper. Preheat the oven to 350°F. Gently melt the butter in a small saucepan, stir in the cocoa until blended and set aside. Beat the eggs and superfine sugar until light then stir in the cocoa mixture. Stir in the vanilla extract, then sift the flour over the mixture by thirds, folding in with a metal spoon after each addition. Turn into the prepared pan and bake in the center of the oven for 40–45 minutes. Leave in the pan for several minutes before turning out on to a wire rack. When the cake is cool, wrap in plastic wrap and leave for 24 hours. This is not essential but makes slicing the cake easier. With a long thin sharp knife, using a sawing motion, slice the cake in half, then slice each half again — making 4 discs. Use a spatula to help keep the discs intact when you remove them. Whip the cream and sandwich between the layers and over the surface of the cake.

To make curls: Stir the chocolate and oil in a double saucepan over hot but not boiling water until smooth. Pour on to a marble or other non-porous surface and spread out with a palette knife into a thinnish layer. Before the chocolate becomes too hard angle the blade of a straight knife and scrape across the chocolate to make curls for decorating the top of the cake. They can be stored in an air-tight container.

Black and White Pound Cake

There is nothing nicer than an old-fashioned pound cake with its lovely buttery taste. It keeps well but you will find it far too tempting to last any time at all.

3oz semi-sweet chocolate, chopped
2 cups self-rising flour
9 tbsp butter, softened
1¼ cups superfine sugar
4 large eggs, room temperature
1 tsp vanilla extract
Serves 10–12

Preheat the oven to 350°F. Butter and flour a 1-qt tubular mold. Sift the flour twice and set aside. Melt the chocolate in a double saucepan over hot but not boiling water and set aside. Cream the butter, then beat in the sugar until light and fluffy. Mix the eggs with the vanilla and very gradually add to the butter mixture. Using a metal spoon, fold the flour into the mixture a quarter at a time. Spoon half the mixture into the mold. Mix the melted chocolate into the remaining cake mixture and spoon into the mold. Plunge a knife into the batter and make several swirling movements to marbleize. Bake for about 50 minutes – until just cooked through. Leave in the mold for 10 minutes before turning out on to a wire rack to cool. Store in an airtight container.

Celestial Tart

A rich, thin, very chocolaty cake that is glazed with chocolate and served warm with poached kumquats.

Kumquats:	3^1/$_2$oz unsweetened
1 lb kumquats	cooking chocolate
^{3}/$_4$ cup sugar	6 tbsp unsalted butter
1^1/$_3$ cups water	**Glaze:**
Cake:	4^1/$_2$oz unsweetened
4 tbsp cake flour	chocolate
^{3}/$_4$ cup superfine sugar	pat of butter
3 large eggs	2 tbsp milk

Serves 8–10

Wash and halve the kumquats lengthwise. Place in a pan with the sugar and water. Simmer gently for 30 minutes and set aside.

Grease an 8 inch shallow round cake pan and line with baking parchment. Using an electric whisk, beat the flour, sugar, and eggs for about 10 minutes. Meanwhile melt the chocolate and butter in a double boiler over barely simmering water. Add this to the egg mixture and continue to whisk for another 10 minutes. Pour into the pan and bake in an oven preheated to 300°F. Bake for 20–25 minutes. Remove from the oven and rest in the pan for 10 minutes. Melt the glaze ingredients together in a double boiler. Turn the cake out on to a wire rack and pour over the melted glaze. Place a plate underneath to catch the drips. Serve lukewarm with a few kumquats spooned over each slice.

Chocolate Fudge Pie

A gorgeous, moist chocolate filling set off by thin, crisp nut pastry.

Pastry:	Filling:
1/2 cup skinned hazelnuts, finely ground	*4oz/125g semi-sweet chocolate*
1 1/2 cups sifted all-purpose flour	*4 tbsp butter*
8 tbsp lightly salted butter, chilled and diced	*2 large eggs*
3 tbsp vanilla superfine sugar	*1/2 cup vanilla superfine sugar*
1 egg, lightly beaten	*2 tbsp flour, sifted*
1–3 tbsp iced water	*4 tbsp heavy cream*
	1 1/2 tbsp rum or brandy

To serve:
grated chocolate or curls (p. 23)
3/4 cup heavy cream
1 tbsp confectioners' sugar (optional)
1 tbsp rum or brandy (optional)
Serves 8

Make pastry by rubbing butter into flour, add hazelnuts and sugar, mix to a stiff dough with egg and water. Refrigerate for 25 minutes then roll out and line a 1 1/2 inch deep 9 inch diameter tart pan with a removable base. Meanwhile preheat the oven to 375°F. Bake blind for about 25 minutes, removing the paper and weights for the last 10 minutes. Cool on a rack while you make the filling.

Melt the chocolate and butter together in the top of a double saucepan and allow to cool. Beat the eggs and sugar together in a large bowl set over hot water. Whisk for about 10 minutes until the mixture forms a ribbon trail when the whisk is lifted. Sift the flour over the top and fold in, then fold in the chocolate mixture. Lastly fold in the cream and alcohol. Pour into the pastry case and bake on a hot baking sheet for 20 minutes. Cool. Remove from

the tin and serve at room temperature, decorate with grated chocolate or curls. Lightly whip the cream, add the sugar and alcohol, and pass separately.

Marbled Cheesecake

This delectable cheesecake looks very handsome with its marbled appearance and has an excellent moist texture.

½ cup cocoa, sifted
2lb cream cheese
½ cup superfine sugar
½ cup vanilla superfine sugar (p. 3)
4 eggs
½ cup crumbled graham crackers,
Serves 12

Preheat the oven to 350°F. Butter an 8 inch diameter, 3 inch deep cake pan and line the bottom with baking parchment. Dissolve the cocoa in 5 tablespoons of hot water and set aside. Using an electric mixer, beat the cheese until it is creamy. Mix in the sugars and then the eggs, one by one. Do not overmix. Pour about half of the mixture into another bowl and stir in the dissolved cocoa. Pour a teacup of the plain mixture into the center of the pan – it will spread out into an even layer. Gently pour a cupful of the dark mixture over the center of the plain mixture and leave it to spread out. Repeat these layers until both mixtures are used up.

Set the cake pan in a roasting dish large enough to contain the pan without touching its sides. Pour boiling water into the roasting dish to come 1½ inch up the sides of the cake pan. Bake for 1½ hours or until the top of the cake is golden. It will rise during baking but will sink later. Remove the cake from the oven and water bath and leave in the pan on a rack to cool. Slip a knife around the edge of the cake. Place a plate upside down over the cake and invert the cake on to the plate. Sprinkle the cookies evenly over the base and gently place another plate over the crumbs and invert again. Cover the cake with plastic wrap and refrigerate. Serve at room temperature in slices, cut with a knife dipped first in hot water and dried.

Chocolate Cheesecake Pie

This can be whipped up in minutes and will please both chocolate and cheesecake fans.

Crust:	**Filling:**
6 oz graham crackers	*11oz cream cheese*
1oz amaretti cookies	*1 cup superfine sugar*
4 tbsp melted butter	*¹/₂ cup cocoa powder sifted*
	¹/₂ tsp cinnamon
	3 eggs
	4 tbsp heavy cream

Serves 8

Preheat the oven to 350°F. Crush all the cookies in a blender, food processor, or with a rolling pin. Put them in a bowl and mix them with the melted butter. Press the crumbs into the bottom of a 9 inch loose-based tart pan. Bake for 10 minutes and then place on a rack to cool.

Using an electric beater, whisk the cheese until it is creamy and smooth and then beat in the sugar, cocoa, and cinnamon. Beat in the eggs one at a time until just blended. Pour into the flan ring and bake the pie for 25–30 minutes or until the filling is puffed up. (It will sink as it cools.) Cool on a rack and serve at room temperature.

Chocolate Velvet Mousse

Chocolate mousse is an all-time favorite but you can ring the changes by serving it in scoops on a sea of pistachio sauce.

5oz unsweetened chocolate
3 egg yolks
5 tbsp unsalted butter, cut into small pieces
1 tbsp crème de cacao, Tia Maria or liqueur of your choice
4 egg whites
3 tbsp vanilla sugar (p. 3)
pinch of salt

Pistachio sauce:
3oz shelled pistachio nuts
1oz blanched almonds
$1/3$ cup vanilla superfine sugar (p. 3)
$1^1/4$ cups milk
3 egg yolks
1–2 drops of green food coloring (optional)

Serves 6

Melt the chocolate in a double boiler set over hot water. Remove from the heat and beat in the egg yolks, one at a time. Stir in the butter and when the mixture is smooth, add the liqueur. Whisk the egg whites with a pinch of salt until stiff, add the sugar and whisk until the whites form stiff peaks. Using a metal spoon, fold a dollop of whites into the chocolate mixture to lighten it and then fold in the remaining whites, incorporating as much air as possible. Turn into an 8 inch dish, cover, and refrigerate until set, about 4 hours.

To make the sauce: Blanch the pistachio nuts in boiling water for 1 minute. Drain, then rub them between a tea cloth to remove some of the skins. Blend or process the pistachios and almonds with a few tablespoons of sugar, then add a few tablespoons of milk and blend to a smooth paste. Heat the remaining milk with the nut paste to just below boiling point. Cover and leave to infuse for 15 minutes. Reheat the milk again to just below boiling point. Whisk the egg yolks with the remaining sugar and then whisk in the hot milk. Return the mixture to the pan and cook over a very low heat, stirring with a wooden spoon, until the custard slightly thickens. Do not allow it to come to a boil or it will curdle. Strain the sauce into a bowl and add the coloring. You might want to add some of the pistachio purée to give the sauce texture.

To serve, pour some sauce on to individual plates. Dip a serving spoon in hot water and then dip the spoon into the mousse to make an oval-shaped scoop. Place a scoop round-side up on the pistachio sauce.

Petits Pôts de Crème au Chocolat

Satin-smooth chocolate custards that do not even have to be baked because the chocolate "seizes" when it is stirred into the boiling cream, and thickens it.

1¼ cups heavy cream
6oz semi-sweet chocolate, chopped
1 tbsp of a fruit eau-de-vie, such as Poire William

Bring the cream to a good boil, remove from the heat and whisk in the chopped chocolate. When the mixture is smooth, stir in the *eau-de-vie*. Divide between four ramekins and place in the refrigerator for a few hours to set.

Panettone Surprise

At Christmas time, Italian foodstores are crowded with boxes containing *panettone* – a light *brioche*-style cake dotted with dried fruit. It is very good toasted or served as is but you can make a very delicious dessert by stuffing it with a *ricotta* and chocolate filling.

2 lb panettone
4 tbsp brandy
1 lb ricotta

3 tbsp superfine sugar
3oz chopped mixed candied peel
5oz semi-sweet chocolate, chopped
Serves 12

Slice a circle from the base of the *panettone* and set aside. Scoop out the inside, leaving a 1½ inch wall. Sprinkle the inside with the brandy. Mix the remaining ingredients together and use to fill the hollow. Replace the base, turn right side up and serve lightly chilled.

Hot Chocolate Soufflé

A chocolate soufflé is always a spectacular and much appreciated dessert. This recipe does not contain any flour and results in a lighter-than-usual version.

4oz unsweetened chocolate,
chopped
⅔ cup heavy cream
3 egg yolks
2 tbsp Grand Marnier,
Cointreau or Curaçao

a pat of butter
5 egg whites
4 tbsp superfine sugar
a pinch of salt
¾ cup light cream

Serves 4

Preheat the oven to 400°F. Butter and sugar a 2-pint soufflé dish. Melt the chocolate and cream together in a heavy-bottomed saucepan over very gentle heat. Remove the pan from the heat and beat in the egg yolks, one at a time. Stir in the liqueur. Whisk the egg whites and salt together until stiff. Add the sugar and continue to whisk until the mixture turns glossy. Fold a few tablespoons of the whites into the chocolate mixture to lighten it. Add this mixture to the remaining whites and fold together carefully. Spoon the mixture into the prepared dish and bake for 12–14 minutes. Lightly whip the cream and serve separately.

Chocolate Soufflé Glacé

You won't have to worry about these soufflés rising! They can be made well in advance and the freezer does the cooking and storing.

¼ cup cocoa powder
2oz semi-sweet chocolate, chopped
2 egg whites
½ cup water
½ cup vanilla superfine sugar (p. 3)
2 tbsp Grand Marnier or a fruit eau-de-vie
1¼ cups heavy cream, lightly whipped
chocolate curls (p. 23)
Serves 4

Prepare individual ramekins by wrapping a collar of baking parchment around each one to extend 1½ inch above the top of the dish and tape this in place. Melt the cocoa, chocolate and 4 tablespoons of water together in the top of a double saucepan set over hot but not boiling water and put aside. Whisk the egg whites until stiff. In a heavy-bottomed small saucepan dissolve the sugar in the remaining water, bring to the boil and boil hard for 3 minutes without stirring. Pour the hot sugar syrup in a steady stream over the whites, while continuing to whisk and keep whisking until the mixture is thick and cool, about 8 minutes. Use a large metal spoon to fold the chocolate into the whites and then fold in the liqueur and whipped cream. Spoon into the ramekins and freeze for at least 3 hours until firm. The soufflés can be frozen for 2 weeks if completely wrapped. Before serving, remove the ramekins from the freezer and leave them in the refrigerator for about 1½ hours to soften. Peel away the paper collars and decorate with chocolate curls before serving.

Marbled Brownies

A scrumptious variation on the irresistible classic brownie.

8oz semi-sweet chocolate, chopped
10 tbsp butter
6 eggs
1¹/₂ cups sugar
1 tsp baking powder
pinch of salt
1 cup flour
3 tsps vanilla extract
6oz cream cheese
Makes 16 squares

Melt chocolate and 6 tablespoons of the butter in the top of a double saucepan. Beat 4 eggs with ³/₄ cup of sugar until light and fluffy. Stir in the chocolate mixture. Set aside 2 tablespoons of the flour. Fold the remaining flour, salt and baking powder into the egg mixture. Add 2 teaspoons of the vanilla extract. Cream the remaining 4 tablespoons of butter with the cream cheese. Add the remaining sugar, 2 eggs, 2 tablespoons of flour and 1 teaspoon of vanilla extract. Line a 9 x 13 inch baking pan with baking parchment. Spread half the chocolate batter in the pan. Pour the cheese mixture over the top. Drop large spoonfuls of the remaining chocolate batter on to the cheese. Swirl (not too much – better if large areas of each are left). Bake in a preheated oven at 350°F for 35 minutes. Do not overbake. The brownies will firm up as they cool. Leave in the pan until cool before cutting into squares.

Brownies

Cocoa is a good substitute for unsweetened chocolate in this recipe.

8 tbsp butter
¹/₂ cup cocoa powder
2 eggs
1 cup superfine sugar
1 tsp vanilla extract
4 tbsp flour
¹/₂ cup of chopped walnuts
Makes 16 squares

Grease an 8 inch square, shallow cake pan and line the bottom with greased wax paper. Preheat the oven to 350°F. Gently melt the butter in a small saucepan, stir in the cocoa until blended and set aside. In a medium-size bowl, beat the eggs and superfine sugar until light, then add the cocoa mixture. Stir in the vanilla extract, then stir in the flour. Fold in the nuts and turn into the prepared pan. Bake in the center of the oven for 30–35 minutes. Do not overcook. Brownies firm up as they cool. Allow to cool completely in the pan before cutting into 2 inch squares. The squares should be quite soft and moist inside.

Tollhouse Cookies

In the last century in America, when it was necessary to ford rivers or cross remote bridges, a toll had to be paid. It was possible to buy refreshments in the house of the toll man – hence the name of these now world-wide popular cookies.

8 tbsp butter
¹/₄ cup vanilla superfine sugar (p. 3)
¹/₂ cup soft dark brown sugar
1 egg
¹/₂ tsp vanilla essence
1 cup plus 2 level tbsp all-purpose flour
¹/₂ tsp baking soda
5oz semi-sweet chocolate,
cut into pea-size pieces
¹/₂ cup chopped walnuts (optional)
Makes about 60

Preheat the oven to 350°F and grease 2 baking sheets. Cream the butter, beat in the two sugars and mix until the consistency is light and fluffy. Lightly mix the egg and vanilla and gradually add to the creamed ingredients. Sift the flour with the bicarbonate of soda and stir it into the mixture. Stir in the chocolate pieces and nuts.

Drop by teaspoons, well spaced out, on to the baking sheets and bake the cookies for 10–12 minutes. Remove immediately with a spatula to a cool flat surface. They will crisp as they cool. If you want a thinner and crisper cookie, add 2–3 tbsp of cold water to the dough. Store the cookies in an airtight tin when cold.

Chocolate Citrus Batons

Chocolate has an affinity with citrus fruit and a delicious sweet can be made by combining the two. Keep a box handy to serve as a treat with after-dinner coffee.

peel from 2 large, thin-skinned grapefruit (or other citrus
fruit), well washed
1¼ cups sugar
8oz semi-sweet chocolate, chopped

Remove the peel in quarters from the fruit. Boil the peel for 15 minutes in enough water to cover. Drain, cover with fresh water and boil again. Repeat until the peel is tender. Drain the peel again and cut into thin baton shapes.

Place the sugar and ½ cup of water in a small heavy-bottomed saucepan and heat until the sugar is dissolved. Add the peel and simmer for about 35 minutes, until the syrup is completely absorbed. Drain the peel, then place on a rack and leave in a dry place overnight.

Melt the chocolate in the top of a double boiler over hot but not boiling water. Spear the pieces of candied fruit with toothpicks and dip into the chocolate. Stick the toothpicks in a large potato or place over the edge of a rack to dry. When dry, remove the toothpicks and store the batons in an air-tight container layered with baking parchment.

Chocolate Cookies

A good, very chocolaty cookie which is crisp outside and chewy inside.

4 egg whites
2½ cups confectioners' sugar
⅓ cup cocoa powder
2 tbsp flour
1 tsp powdered instant coffee
1 tbsp water
scant cup of whole walnuts, very finely chopped
(makes 18)

Preheat the oven to 350°F. Line a baking sheet with baking parchment. Using an electric beater, whisk the egg whites until frothy. Add the sugar, cocoa, flour, coffee and water to the bowl and beat first at a slow speed and then at a higher speed for a few minutes until the mixture thickens. Fold in the walnuts. Place tablespoons of the mixture on the prepared baking sheet leaving a 1 inch space between each spoonful. Bake for 15 minutes. The top will be firm and cracked but the inside still soft. Lift off the cookies and place them on a rack to cool.

Chocolate Truffles

These velvety-textured truffles melt in the mouth and are just the thing to serve with after-dinner coffee. Good chocolate (essential for this recipe) is costly but store-bought truffles are far more expensive and often less good.

1 cup light cream
2 tbsp butter
1 vanilla bean
1 lb semi-sweet chocolate, chopped
2 tbsp rum or brandy or liqueur of your choice (optional)
Coatings:
4 tbsp cocoa
2 tbsp confectioners' sugar
chocolate sprinkles
finely chopped nuts

Heat the cream with the butter and vanilla bean until it reaches a rolling boil. Remove from the heat and lift out the vanilla bean (this can be rinsed off, dried, and put in a jar of sugar for flavoring).

Meanwhile melt the chocolate in the top of a double boiler over hot but not boiling water. Mix the chocolate into the cream and add the alcohol if you are using it. Pour into a shallow pan lined with baking parchment and spread out with a palette knife. Leave in a cool place, uncovered, for 24 hours.

Pull off small pieces of chocolate and roll into balls on the palms of your hands. Mix the cocoa and confectioners' sugar. Roll the truffles in this mixture, or in the chocolate, or in the nuts. Keep the truffles refrigerated in a covered container layered with baking parchment.

White Chocolate Ice Cream

This ice cream captures the flavor of white chocolate and is exceedingly good served with a bitter chocolate sauce (p.59).

5oz white chocolate, chopped
1¹/₃ cups milk
¹/₃ cup vanilla superfine sugar (p. 3)
2 cups heavy cream
(makes 4–5 cups)

Place the chocolate with 4 tablespoons of milk in the top of a double saucepan set over hot but not boiling water. Cover and leave to melt. Meanwhile dissolve the sugar in the remaining milk over gentle heat. Allow the milk to cool to room temperature before stirring in the melted chocolate. Lightly whip the cream and fold into the chocolate mixture. Freeze in an ice cream maker or in the fast freeze section of a freezer.

White Chocolate Truffles

These are easy to make and look spectacular when arranged with dark chocolate truffles.

6oz white chocolate, chopped
5 tbsp unsalted butter, diced
3 tbsp heavy cream
1 tsp orange liqueur
a pinch of salt

Place the chocolate, butter, cream and salt in the top of a double boiler set over barely simmering water and stir until the mixture is smooth. Remove from the heat and add the liqueur. Cover and refrigerate until firm, about 2 hours. Pull off marble-size pieces and roll them in the palms of your hands to shape into balls. If the mixture becomes difficult to handle, return to the refrigerator and chill further. Store refrigerated in a covered container layered with baking parchment.

Chocolate Ice Cream with
White Chocolate Truffles

Dark, creamy, chocolate ice cream mixed with white truffles makes a spectacular chocolate treat.

> *6oz semi-sweet chocolate*
> *2 cups milk*
> *5 egg yolks*
> *$1/2$ cup vanilla superfine sugar (p. 3)*
> *$1^1/4$ cups heavy cream, lightly whipped*
> *small white truffles (p. 55)*
> **(makes about 2 cups)**

Melt the chocolate in the top of a double saucepan and set aside. Bring the milk to just below the boil. Whisk the egg yolks with the sugar in a bowl until thick and light and then whisk in the hot milk. Return the mixture to the saucepan and stir continually with a wooden spoon over gently heat until the custard thickens enough to just coat the spoon. Do not allow it to boil or it will curdle. Stir in the melted chocolate and strain into a bowl. Refrigerate until cool and then fold in the lightly whipped cream. Turn the mixture into an ice cream maker. When the ice cream is made, remove it from the machine and fold in the truffles. Freeze until ready to use. Leave at room temperature for about 20 minutes to soften before serving.

Sauces

CHOCOLATE

½ cup heavy cream
2 tbsp butter
½ cup cocoa, sifted
¼ cup superfine sugar
⅓ cup brown sugar
pinch of salt
Makes about 1 cup

Place all the ingredients in a heavy saucepan and stir over a low heat until the mixture is smooth. Add more sugar if you want a sweeter sauce.

BITTER CHOCOLATE

3½oz unsweetened chocolate
2 tbsp butter
5 tbsp water
1 tbsp rum or brandy
Makes about1 cup

Melt the first 3 ingredients together in a small heavy-bottomed saucepan over a gentle heat, stirring continuously. Do not allow it to boil. Stir in the alcohol and serve warm or cold.

CHOCOLATE RUM RAISIN

Soak some raisins in rum for several hours and add to the Bitter Chocolate sauce as above. Flavor the sauce with 1 tablespoon rum (omit brandy).

Index